Creativity, reflection, practical wisdom and encouragement
for the trauma informed parent

FOSTER & ADOPTIVE PARENTING

JESS DANAE ROBINSON

tellwell

Tellwell Talent
www.tellwell.ca

ISBN
978-0-2288-9563-3 (Hardcover)
978-0-2288-9564-0 (Paperback)

For my husband and children: You have my whole heart. You are the most beautiful part of my life.

Special Thanks

To author Bessel Van der Kolk for his compelling work in "The Body Keeps the Score: Brain, Mind, and Body in the Healing of Trauma". With permission I have shared his work throughout this book.

DEAR PARENT,

YOU HAVE CREATED SPACE IN YOUR HOME; YOU HAVE CREATED SPACE IN YOUR FAMILY FOR A HURTING CHILD. IN DOING SO, YOU HAVE CHOSEN A LIFE THAT MAKES YOU VERY VULNERABLE, A LIFE YOU HOLD VERY LITTLE CONTROL OVER, A LIFE THAT CAN BE VERY ANXIETY-INDUCING, OVERWHELMING, DYSREGULATING, EXHAUSTING, AND PAINFUL. YOU HAVE ALSO CHOSEN A LIFE WITH SO MUCH BEAUTY AND POSSIBILITY IN YOUR DAILY PURPOSE, A LIFE THAT WILL EXPAND YOUR HEART IN WAYS YOU NEVER KNEW WERE POSSIBLE, A LIFE THAT BEHOLDS MIRACLES, LOVES BIG, AND EXPERIENCES DEEP JOY. PARENT, WHAT YOU ARE DOING EVERY DAY MATTERS SO MUCH. YOUR ORDINARY DAY HOLDS PRECIOUS SIGNIFICANCE. I HOPE YOU FEEL VALUED, SEEN, AND NEEDED. I CREATED THESE COLOURING PAGES FOR YOU TO ENJOY ALONGSIDE YOUR CHILD WHILE THEY ARE INDEPENDENTLY PLAYING, FOR YOU TO ENJOY WITH YOUR CHILD SO YOU CAN WORK ON SOMETHING TOGETHER, OR FOR YOUR OWN PERSONAL ENJOYMENT. I HAVE FOUND CREATIVITY TO BE A GREAT FORM OF SELF-REGULATION IN MY OWN FOSTER/ADOPTIVE PARENTING. I USE COLOURING

FREQUENTLY TO SUPPORT MY BODY IN CALMING DOWN IN DIFFICULT MOMENTS. I ALSO USE COLOURING TO ENCOURAGE INDEPENDENT PLAY FOR MY CHILDREN. I HAVE SHARED PRACTICAL WISDOM THROUGHOUT THIS BOOK TO SURROUND YOU WHILE PARENTING A CHILD WITH TRAUMA. I HOPE THIS BOOK SERVES YOU AS YOU PROCESS YOUR UNIQUE PARENTING JOURNEY. I HOPE IT PROVIDES WISDOM AND GUIDANCE FOR CULTIVATING FAMILY ROUTINES, AND I HOPE IT ENCOURAGES YOU IN WHAT YOU ARE ALREADY DOING. I HAVE CREATED OPPORTUNITIES FOR JOURNAL REFLECTIONS AND MY FAVOURITE PARENTING IDEAS FOR SUPPORTING REGULATION. USE WHAT IS MOST HELPFUL AND DOABLE FOR YOU; DISREGARD WHAT ISN'T. I HOPE THIS BOOK PROVIDES YOU WITH AN EASY-TO-GRAB RESOURCE TO ALLEVIATE DISTRESS, UNDO ISOLATION OR HOPELESSNESS, AND FUEL FOR YOU AS YOU PARENT. YOU ARE DOING SUCH IMPORTANT WORK. YOU ARE NOT ALONE.

JESS

About the Author

Jess has spent years supporting a wide range of people who have experienced childhood trauma, crisis and dysregulation. Jess is a foster and adoptive mama. She lives with her husband and children in Ontario. Jess and her husband Cody hold a strong passion for building attachment, supporting regulation, and providing trauma-informed care within their home and family. She enjoys the humbling and tender process of learning, creativity, adjusting, and growing when it comes to her own parenting journey.

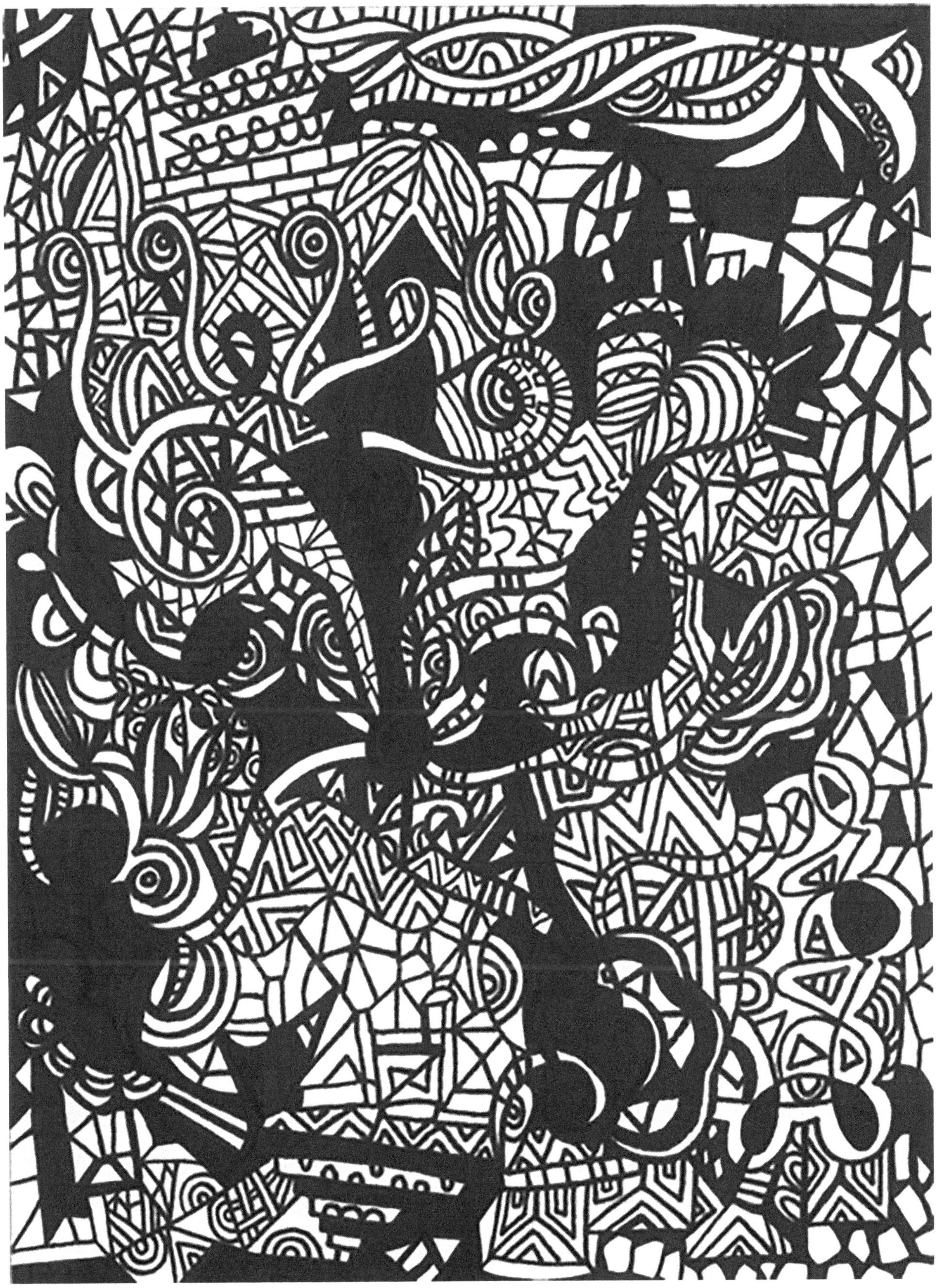

"Traumatized people chronically feel unsafe inside their bodies: The past is alive in the form of gnawing interior discomfort. Their bodies are constantly bombarded by visceral warning signs, and, in an attempt to control these processes, they often become expert at ignoring their gut feelings and in numbing awareness of what is played out inside. They learn to hide from their selves."
— Bessel A. van der Kolk

You may need
Downtime
A screen
To be with me
Jammies
To relax

You may need
Comfort
Burgers and ice cream
Stuffies in tow
To wrap up
To be cozy

You may need
Outside
The forest
Paths to walk; you lead
A swing at the park
Repetition

You may need
Water
A sink full of bubbles
A sensory bath
To dip your feet
In the lake

You may need
A long bedtime
To hear a voice singing
Storytelling
Arms rocking
The lamp on all night

You may need
Inside
Creativity
Free play
Time to pretend
Imagination

You may need
Slow
Slow morning
Slow afternoon
Slow evening
Calm

You may need
Me
To get creative
To explore your needs
Your safety in determining rhythm
As long as you need

Photo by Cody Robinson

Reflection

How do you know when your child is not feeling safe?

How can you build more intentional felt safety into your child's life?

What unsafe experiences or unsafe situations has your child gone through, witnessed, or been exposed too?

What helps you feel safe as the caregiver? How can you build more intentional felt safety into your life?

Supporting Regulation

Use a bath or a shower to support regulation and felt safety. Use bubbles, salts, toys, water crayons, sensory items (example pom-poms), and nice music. Include their favourite snack and a drink to enjoy during the bath. Try building baths or showers into a regular routine not just for cleaning but for supporting regulation. If your child finds being alone a struggle or it is not safe to do so, try sitting on the bathroom floor and reading a book to yourself, or sit outside the bathroom so they know you are close and available.

Use water to support your regulation as a parent. Take an extended shower or prepare a bath with bubbles, salts, wine, chocolate, a TV show, or nice music. Visit the beach, hike near a stream, or enjoy some spa time with a good book or a journal.

Journal

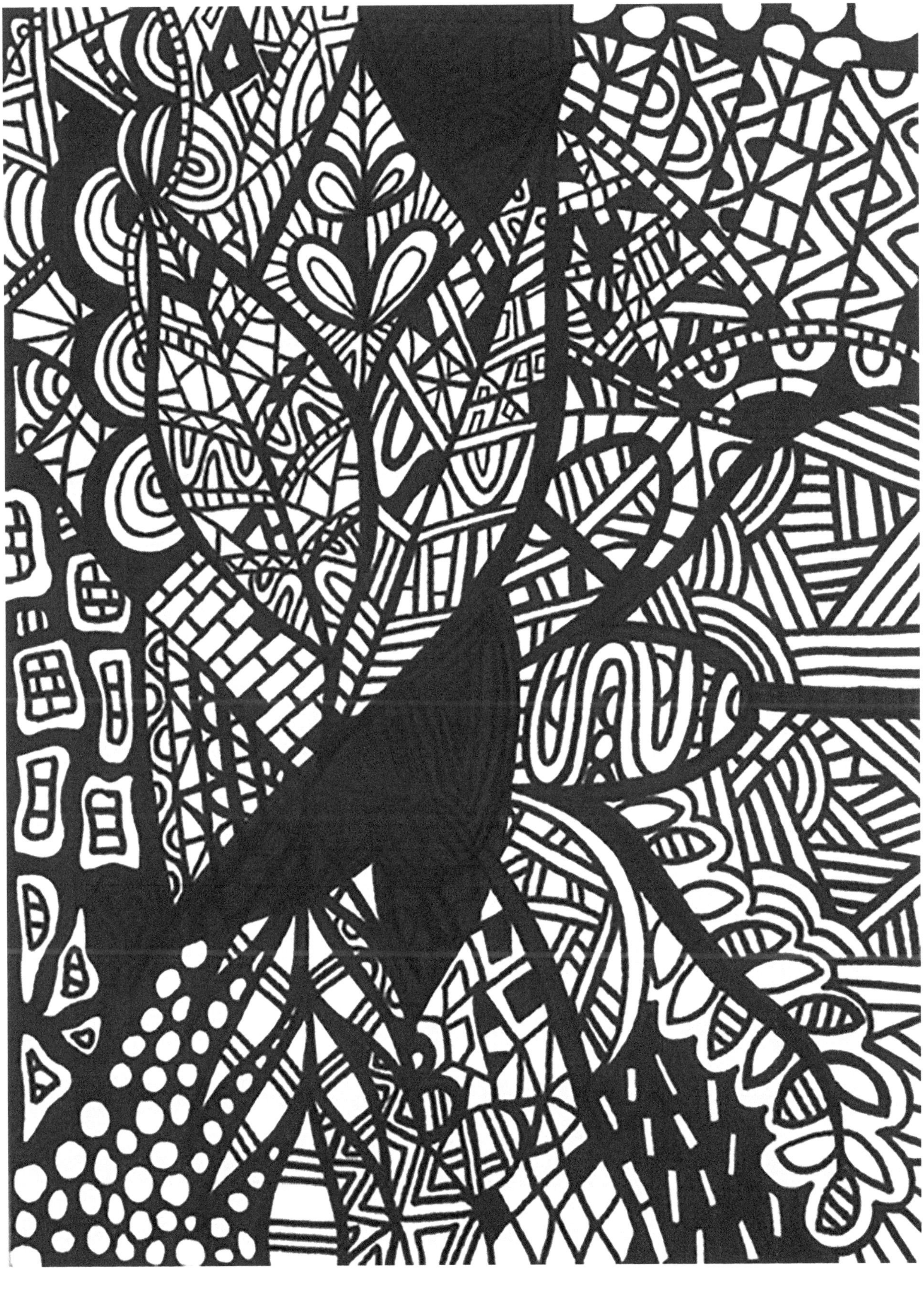

"Being able to feel safe with other people is probably the single most important aspect of mental health; safe connections are fundamental to meaningful and satisfying lives."
— Bessel A. van der Kolk

Photo by Cody Robinson

Offer your child options for how to physically engage with others around them. Try to alleviate any pressure or guilt. Physical choices can provide agency, healing, growth, and repair. "Would you like to give a hug, a high five, a smile, or a wave?" All children benefit from knowing it is their choice to be touched and how they would like to be touched. It's helpful to share clear specifics regarding the physical boundaries you as the parent have already set for them. Come up with a couple of consistent sentences that they will be able to memorize for themselves and do check-ins with you such as "Nobody looks at or touches my bum, vagina, penis, or chest. I don't look at or touch anyone else's bum, vagina, penis, or chest. If I need help with my body, I only get help from my parents or the doctor. If someone crosses my body boundary or I cross someone else's body boundary, I share with my parents right away. I don't keep secrets from my parents." Children need to know that the people around them are also in charge of their own bodies; they need to learn to respect others' physical boundaries as well. Children need to feel empowered to have good, healthy, and

CONSISTENT COMMUNICATION SURROUNDING THEIR BODIES. I HAVE SEEN THESE FREQUENT PRACTICES OF COMMUNICATION, CHECK-INS, AND DEBRIEFING TO BE SO HEALING AND GROWING FOR CONFIDENCE, SECURITY, TRUST, AND INDEPENDENCE. WHEN THIS PART OF LIFE FEELS CONFUSING AND INSECURE, OR PHYSICAL BOUNDARIES HAVE ALREADY BEEN CROSSED FOR A CHILD, IT BECOMES SO IMPORTANT TO BE VERY INTENTIONAL ABOUT THESE PRACTICES.

Reflection

Did your child have any safe family connections before they came to your home?

If so, are you able to continue that (those) family relationship(s)?

What are you currently doing to build safe connections with your child every day?

Do you currently have your own safe connections?

Supporting Regulation

Sit in your child's bedroom with them. Encourage them to find something to do on their own. Give a few options to choose from if they are stuck. Be with them, quietly focused on your own activity such as colouring, drawing, or reading a book. Allow them to settle, feeling your safety, your regulation, and your calm. If they want to talk or are not settling, quietly remind them you are both taking a break and doing your own activity right now. Then, resume what you are doing.

Journal

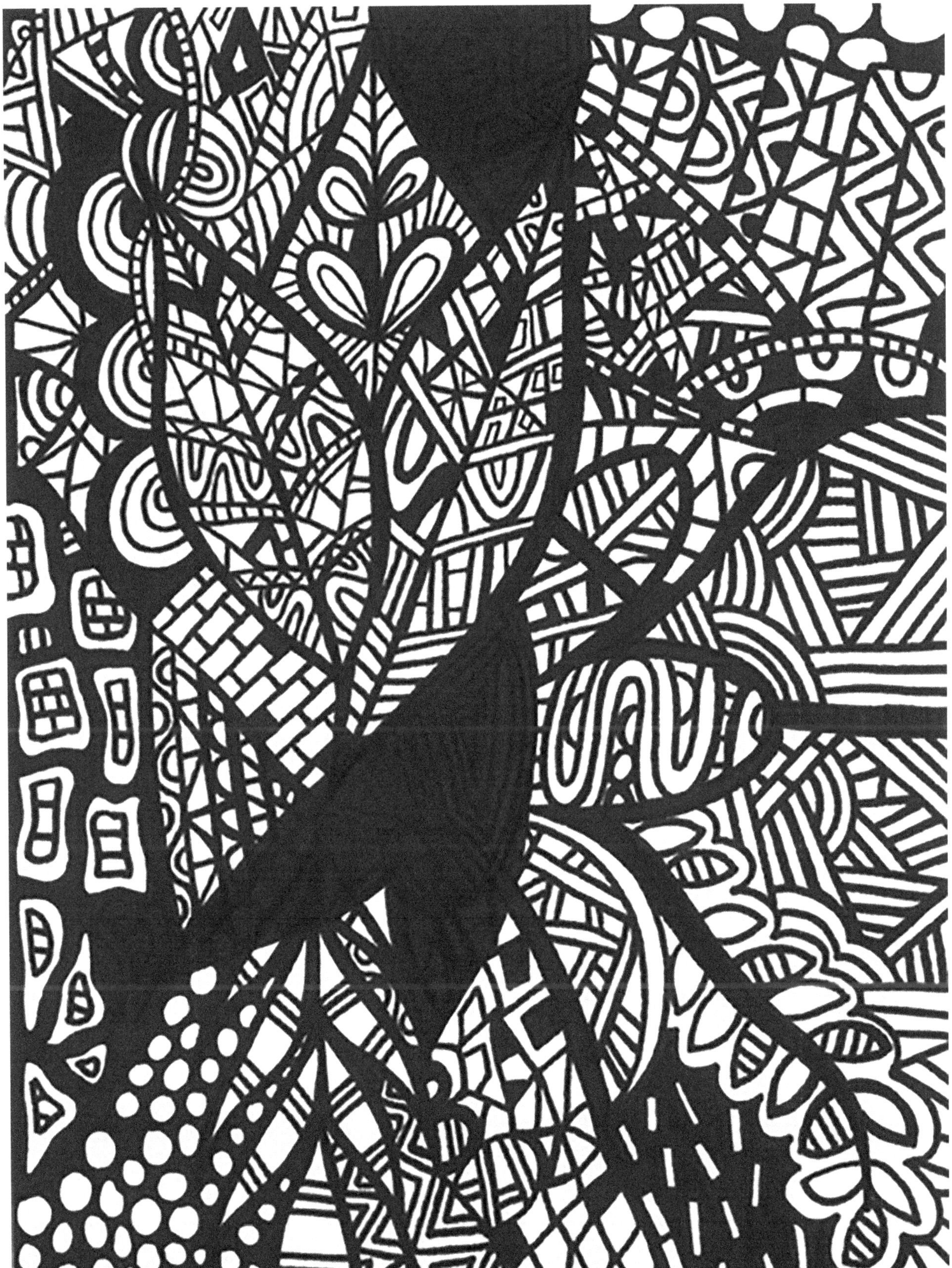

"Long after a traumatic experience is over, it may be reactivated at the slightest hint of danger and mobilize disturbed brain circuits and secrete massive amounts of stress hormones. This precipitates unpleasant emotions, intense physical sensations, and impulsive and aggressive actions. These posttraumatic reactions feel incomprehensible and overwhelming."
— Bessel A. van der Kolk

Little body holding hurt

Little body often misunderstood

Little body carrying grief

Little body constant distress

Little body working so hard

Little body screaming

Little body shaking

Little body pushing

Little body out of control

Little body shutting down

Little body overwhelmed

Little body exhausted

Little body isolated

Little body dissociated

Little body insecure

I WILL HOLD YOU, LITTLE BODY

I WILL COMMIT TO UNDERSTANDING YOU, LITTLE BODY

I WILL CARRY YOU, LITTLE BODY

I WILL BE YOUR CONSTANT, LITTLE BODY

I WILL WORK SO HARD FOR YOU, LITTLE BODY

Photo by Cody Robinson

Reflection

When do you notice your child becoming dysregulated?

When do you notice your child struggling with their emotions?

When do you notice your child becoming aggressive?

What has helped calm their body down in those moments? If nothing has helped so far, what could you do to try to support their body in calming down?

When do you notice yourself becoming dysregulated, struggling with your emotions, or becoming aggressive in your actions?

What has helped in calming your own body down in those moments? If nothing has helped so far, what could you try to support your own body in calming down?

Supporting Regulation

Pick out some items with your child or for your child that encourage calm. Put them in a bag/purse that they can carry around or have access to. These calming items could include snacks or treats, a water bottle, a stuffed animal, sensory items, fidgets, games, art supplies, or a journal. Create your own as well if you find this helpful. Put your items in a basket or a purse to take with you.

Journal

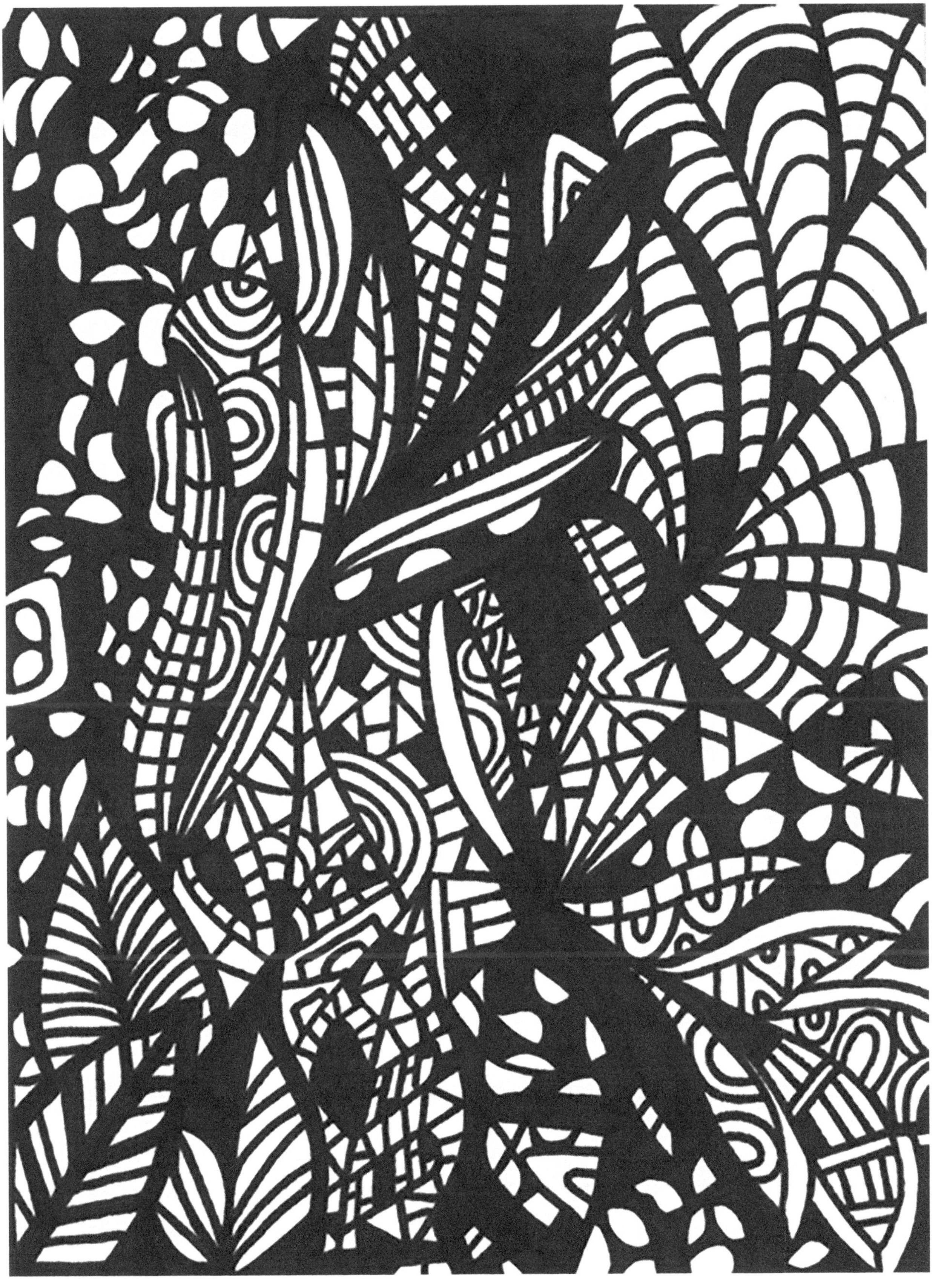

"After trauma, the world is experienced with a different nervous system. The survivor's energy now becomes focused on suppressing inner chaos..."
— Bessel A. van der Kolk

Commit to learning and observing your child's physical cues/tells. What are they outwardly demonstrating of their internal experience? What are they not communicating verbally? Are they revealing potential nervousness, shame, guilt, fear, anxiety, jealousy, anger, loneliness, grief, sadness, overwhelm, confusion, etc.? They may need tangible help from you, depending on what they may be experiencing. They may need to sit with you and squish a stress ball in their fingers or play with a fidget toy. They may need to move energy through their body with you through movement or active play. They may need to wrap up in a weighted blanket. They may need to do some deep breathing exercises with you. They may need a tight hug or your hand rubbing or pressing on their back to secure them. They may need to be rocked back and forth, back and forth, to be soothed. They may need you to pull over the car and let them stretch and move for a few minutes. They may need to be given the opportunity to scream and throw things in a safe way. Depending on the child, try and try again with different ways to intervene and help their body manage their

INTERNAL EXPERIENCES OF DISTRESS. TRY TALKING TO THEM AND ASKING QUESTIONS WHEN IT FEELS APPROPRIATE. SUPPORT THEM IN FINDING LANGUAGE FOR WHAT THEY ARE FEELING AND WHERE THEY FEEL IT IN THEIR BODY SO THAT THEY CAN LEARN HOW TO RESPOND IN A WAY THAT HELPS THEIR NERVOUS SYSTEM.

Photo by Cody Robinson

Reflection

How does reflecting on your child's nervous system affect you?

Knowing how hard your child may be working internally, what might you alter in your family's or your child's daily routine?

Supporting Regulation

Do sensory play together or set it up for them and do your own activity beside them. You could set up creative sand, paint, dough, putty, sensory beads, or baking clay. You could fill up a sink of dishes and soap for them. Do this in intentional silence or put on calming music. If speaking is needed, keep your voice gentle and soothing. If it's a nice day outside, bring a blanket out to the yard, the porch, or the park.

Journal

"How many mental health problems, from drug addiction to self-injurious behaviour, start as attempts to cope with the unbearable physical pain of our emotions?"
— Bessel A. van der Kolk

The Body You Came From

Body holding hurt
Body often misunderstood
Body carrying grief
Body in constant distress
Body working so hard

Body, when have you screamed?
Body, what has shaken you?
Body, how have you pushed away?
Body, how have you been out of control?
Body, how have you shut down?

Body overwhelmed
Body exhausted
Body isolated
Body dissociated
Body insecure

I WILL REMEMBER YOUR BODY
IN THIS CHILD'S STORY
I WILL COMMIT TO UNDERSTANDING YOUR BODY
I WILL SHARE WITH THIS CHILD
WHEN THEY WANT TO KNOW

Photo by Cody Robinson

Reflection

Does your child have any birth family members who live with a mental illness, an addiction, or self-harming behaviours?

How do you view them, think about them, or talk about them with your child?

Is it possible to cultivate compassion for birth family members through understanding these possible roots in their life?

Supporting Regulation

Purchase a membership to an indoor playground, a swimming pool, or a trampoline park, etc. This allows you the freedom to go whenever for however long they need or you need. Allow them to have free time within these spaces where there are few rules, natural boundaries, and a lot of space and options to move their bodies however they need to. Play with them if that is needed. Other times, choose to watch and allow them the independence of being in full control of how they want to play. Avoid taking your phone out. Let them feel the security that you are watching them and interested in what they are doing.

Journal

"Because traumatized people often have trouble sensing what is going on in their bodies, they lack a nuanced response to frustration. They either react to stress by becoming 'spaced out' or with excessive anger."
— Bessel A. van der Kolk

"I have to calm my body" is a consistent phrase said in our family. Every person needs a margin in their days to do physical check-ins when confusing or difficult feelings come up. This can be great modelling for children when we as parents tune in with ourselves in front of them. It can teach them that we are each in charge of our own bodies. Every person has a responsibility to make choices and create good options for themselves. We all need to tend to, nurture, and cultivate the practice of listening and responding carefully to our own bodies.

Photo by Cody Robinson

Reflection

How can you help support your child in sensing what is going on in their body?

How can you tune in with your child when you see or sense that something difficult is going on for them?

How can you support yourself in sensing what is going on in your body?

How can you tune in with yourself when you sense that something difficult is going on for you?

Supporting Regulation

Provide your child with a location wherever you go for them to "take space" if they are having a hard time. This could be their bedroom at home, a space where they can have privacy if they are at someone else's house, pulling over when driving to get them to a safe place if needed, etc. Communicate these locations, and remind them of these locations before being in that setting. If they are mistreating themselves and will allow you to be present, "take space" with them in that spot to help them calm down. If they are mistreating you or the people around them, remind them that they need to "take space" on their own until they are ready to have help calming down without hurting anyone. Stay consistent, asking every few minutes if they are ready to have some help calming down so that they remain in full control and have the choice. Set a consistent boundary with your child that you will not come close to them until they are ready to begin calming down. This reinforces that even in hard moments they are still not allowed to mistreat anyone, including you.

Journal

"Managing your terror all by yourself gives rise to another set of problems: dissociation, despair, addictions, a chronic sense of panic, and relationships that are marked by alienation, disconnections, and explosions."
— Bessel A. van der Kolk

What have you chosen
excessively
to cope?
What have you turned to
repeatedly
to survive?

Food
Bullying
Self-harm
Drugs
Poor hygiene
Sexual behaviour
Thrill-seeking
Pornography
Screens
Acting older
Acting younger
Lying
Stealing

Manipulation
Compliance
Dissociation
Rage
Running away

I want to know
How you have coped?
I want to know
How you have survived?

Your child brings their coping strategies and survival techniques when they join your family. Their challenging behaviours do not define who they are as a person. Commit to learning to view their repelling or negative behaviours through this lens. Seek to move from judgement or fear of their behaviours toward tenderness, compassion, and grace. When children are abused or neglected, they often become desperate. They tend to look for anything they can access to alleviate distress, regardless of the consequences of how harmful it may be for themselves or for others. Expect change, growth, healing, and recovery to be slow and through taking very small steps at a time. Expect to make mistakes as a parent in how you handle difficult parts of their story, their choices, and their behaviours. Commit to repeatedly showing them grace, extending forgiveness, and demonstrating unconditional love and presence to them when they get it wrong. Ask them to show you grace and extend forgiveness to you when you get it wrong.

Photo by Cody Robinson

Reflection

Before coming to your home, in what ways has your child had to cope and survive?

Supporting Regulation

Bring your child to the beach to play in the sand, collect rocks, throw rocks into the water, or sit on a blanket by the water. Bring them to the forest for a hike. Climb a tree. Let them jump into your arms. Go for a bike ride. Go swimming together. Go for a walk around the neighbourhood, allowing them to lead and decide which ways to go. Swing together at the park. Create intentional opportunities to play and enjoy together.

Journal

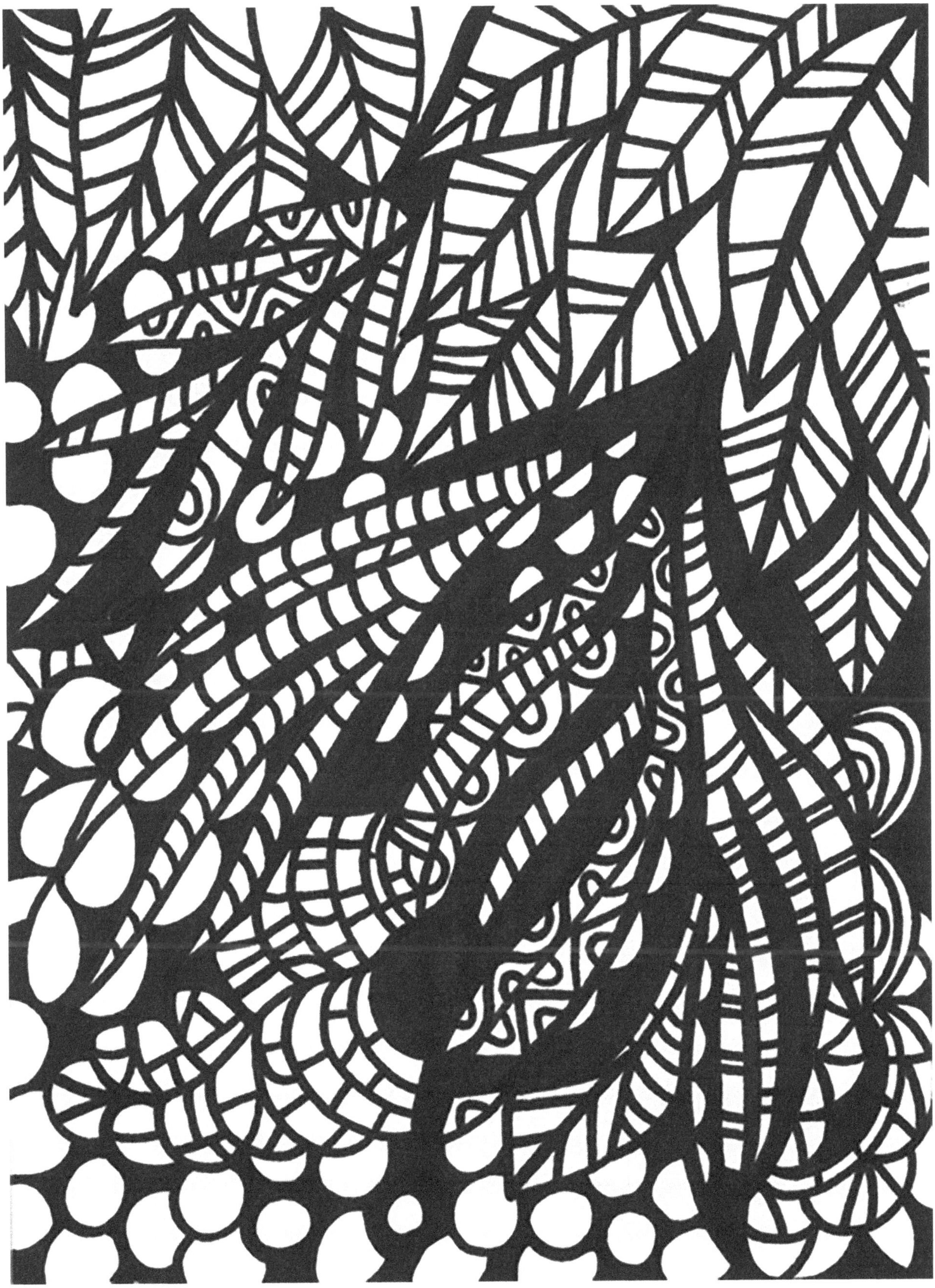

"Children with histories of abuse and neglect learn that their terror, pleading, and crying do not register with their caregiver. Nothing they can do or say stops the beating or brings attention and help. In effect they're being conditioned to give up when they face challenges later in life."
— Bessel A. van der Kolk

Regardless of the age of your child or how independent they may seem, work to build in consistent routines of intentional caregiving. Create daily opportunities to fill in gaps of scarcity they may have experienced in how they were nurtured and nourished in their past. This could look like feeding your child and eating with them, or wrapping your child up in a blanket and rocking them, even if they seem too big. This could look like playing with their hair or brushing it after they have had a shower or a bath. Sing to them. Tuck them in at night. Read aloud to them, and have them read aloud to you.

Photo by Cody Robinson

Reflection

In what ways has your child experienced abuse or neglect?

How does this inform how you parent them?

Are there any adjustments, exceptions, or changes that could be made in how you parent them?

Supporting Regulation

Build predictable routines of pleasure and connection within your home. This nurtures trust and stability for your child. This allows your child to see and experience that there are many times of the day to enjoy and look forward to in the home and with the family. Pleasure is not scarce; there is abundance every day, all throughout the day. Consistency and predictability are key.

Cuddle time. Quiet time. Screen time. Adventure time. Music time. Treat time. Creative time. Storytime. Family time. Friend time. Cooking time. Bath time. Play time. Meal time. Free time. Outside time. Inside time. Game time. Bedtime.

It may seem excessive to create structures like these throughout the day. However, for a child that has not been able to predict much of their life or days, this can bring immense healing, developmental growth, and regulation.

Journal

"Attachment researchers have shown that our earliest caregivers don't only feed us, dress us, and comfort us when we are upset; they shape the way our rapidly growing brain perceives reality. Our interactions with our caregivers convey what is safe and what is dangerous: whom we can count on and who will let us down; what we need to do to get our needs met."
— Bessel A. van der Kolk

Prioritize regular reassurance and information surrounding the schedule for each day. Depending on their age you could use pictures, a calendar, or a daily schedule, or you could simply communicate what they can expect before it happens. Complete the schedule for them or with them and go through the things they can count on for the day. Leave space for asking questions. This will help to build trust and safety around what they can count on each day. It helps to have a number of unchanging pillars every day that they can always count on happening, even if other things need to change.

Photo by Cody Robinson

Reflection

How are you intentionally building attachment with your child?

How has your child been hurt in the area of attachment?

In what ways have you witnessed healthy attachment growing in your home?

Supporting regulation

Nurture your child with food every day. Help with their personal hygiene. Provide predictable safe touch. Play with and brush their hair. Take them shopping for a new outfit or an accessory. Take them out for a dinner or a treat date. Create a predictable bedtime and morning routine with a few different steps they will enjoy each time. Prepare bedtime and morning snacks. If food has been a neglected part of their life, create a food cart or a cupboard they can always have access to day or night in order to heal and build the trust of having all their needs met.

Journal

"Trauma, by definition, is unbearable and intolerable. Most rape victims, combat soldiers, and children who have been molested become so upset when they think about what they experienced that they try to push it out of their minds, trying to act as if nothing happened, and move on. It takes tremendous energy to keep functioning while carrying the memory of terror, and the shame of utter weakness and vulnerability."
— Bessel A. van der Kolk

Take time to reflect on the difficult parts of your child's life and how those difficult parts impact their life now. Reflect on the specific ways they are healing, developing, and growing, regardless of how small or insignificant these ways may seem. It's important to regularly practise noticing the movements and glimmers of hope so that when they are stuck or feeling hopeless, it doesn't overshadow the beauty of their story. After doing this, reflect on the ways you are healing, developing, and growing as a parent to them. Affirm your child verbally all that you are seeing in them often. Seek verbal affirmation from a few people in your life who are committed to seeing you and speaking into your life often.

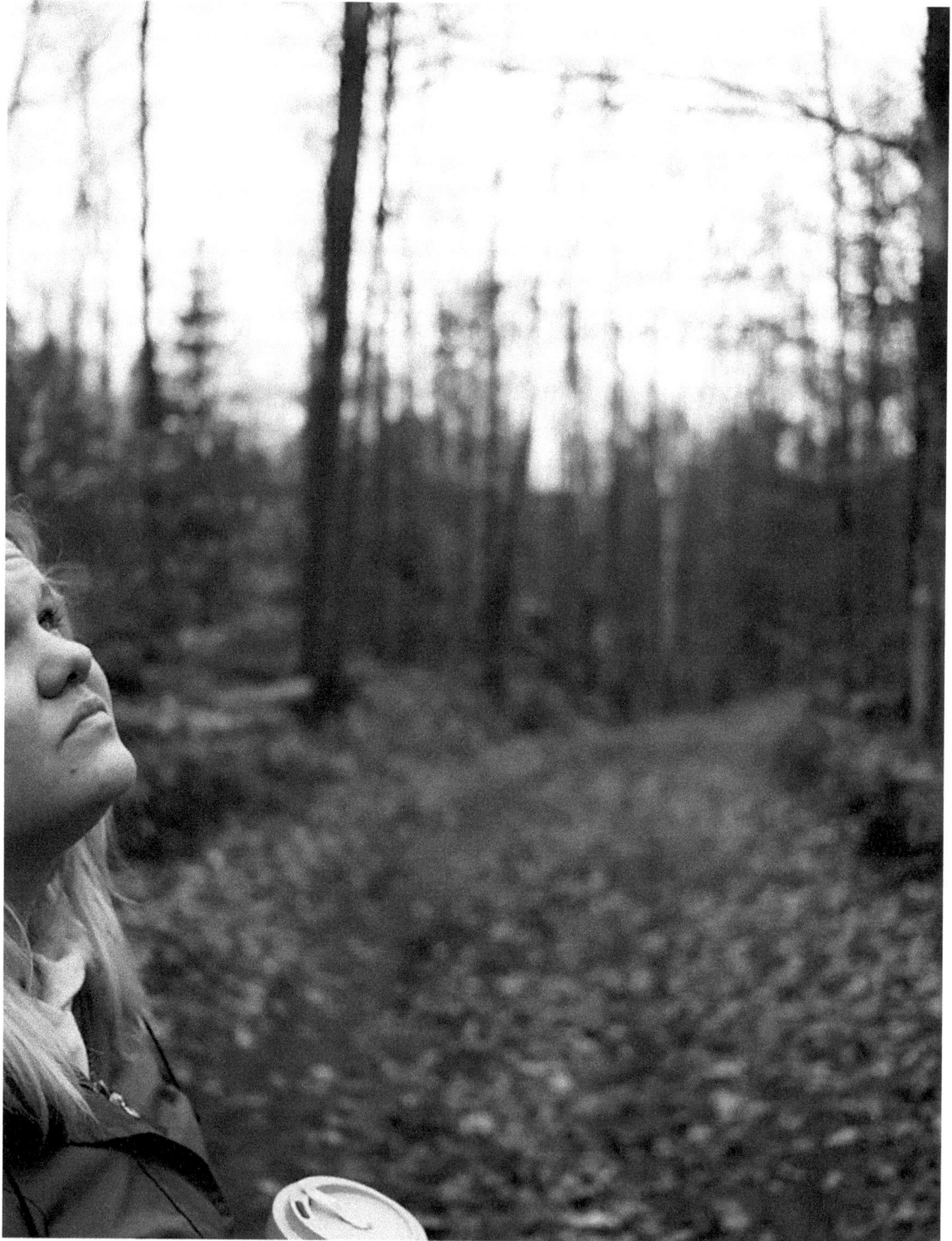

Photo by Cody Robinson

Reflection

What are the details of your child's traumatic experiences?

What steps have you taken to create opportunities of healing for your child? If you haven't yet, what steps might you be able to take?

Have you experienced trauma? What steps have you taken to create opportunities of healing for yourself? If you haven't yet, what steps might you be able to take?

Supporting Regulation

Create screen time as an opportunity for the whole family to relax and decompress together. Provide screen use/phone use in a common area; don't make it accessible in bedrooms or isolated areas. Keep close to your child while they are using a screen. Use this an opportunity for snuggling while sharing snacks or treats. Everyone can be cozy together, winding down together.

Journal

"Under normal conditions people react to a threat with a temporary increase in their stress hormones. As soon as the threat is over, the hormones dissipate and the body returns to normal. The stress hormones of traumatized people, in contrast, take much longer to return to baseline and spike quickly and disproportionately in response to mildly stressful stimuli. The insidious effects of constantly elevated stress hormones include memory and attention problems, irritability, and sleep disorders."
— Bessel A. van der Kolk

What are you willing to alter or change in your life if your child is stuck, declining, or just requiring more support?

What are you willing to do when nothing seems to be helping? Some questions to consider:

Do you need to work less, take a leave, or quit your job altogether?

Do you need to reorganize your budget and shift some priorities around?

Do you need to call your social worker or another trusted person to explore some different options?

Do you need to enrol in an activity together, such as yoga, a music class, an art class, sports, etc.?

Would therapy or coaching be helpful for you or your child or both?

Do you need to consider homeschooling them? Do you need to consider a modified school day/school week?

Do you need to plan a special trip or vacation with them?

Do you need to quit something or slow down to make more room in your schedule?

Do need more help from your support system or community?

Photo by Cody Robinson

Reflection

Knowing how distressed your child may be consistently, what routines would be helpful to build into their day?

Supporting Regulation

Ask yourself, "What will help me enjoy being around my child right now?" Let that inform what you do next when you are feeling angry, irritated, exhausted, or overwhelmed with your child. Pull out a game, a book, an activity, or a craft to do together. Cook something together; do a chore together. Go to the library and read or do an activity together. Go on a walk or a bike ride. Plan a date you will both enjoy. Plan a weekend getaway with them. Drive with the windows down and the music up. When you are struggling to "like" your child, become intentional in bringing you back to a place of liking and enjoying who they are. Create an experience of fun you will both enjoy.

Journal

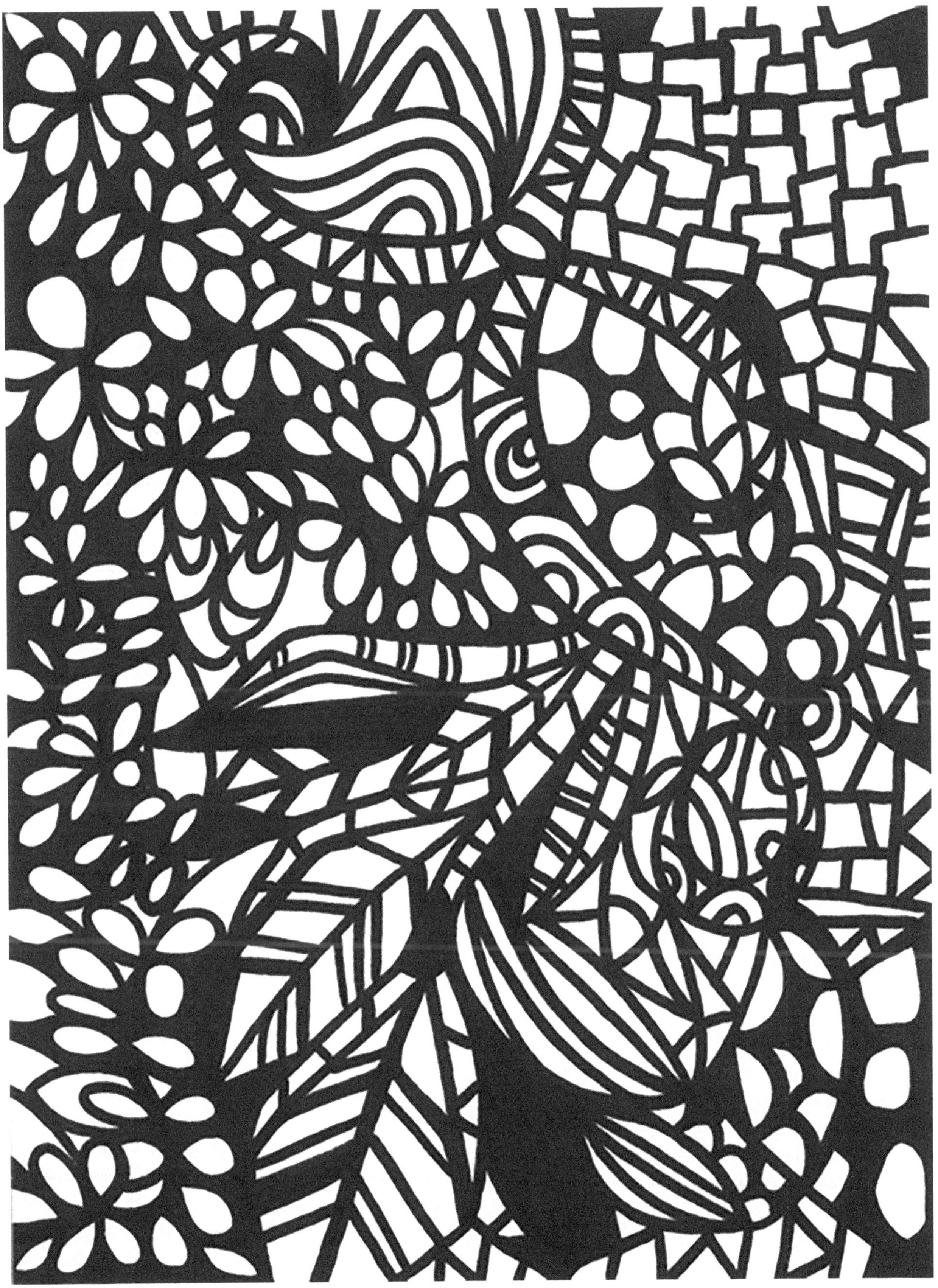

"People can learn to control and change their behaviour, but only if they feel safe enough to experiment with new solutions. The body keeps the score: If trauma is encoded in heartbreaking and gut-wrenching sensations, then our first priority is to help people move out of fight-or-flight states, reorganize their perception of danger, and manage relationships. Where traumatized children are concerned, the last things we should be cutting from school schedules are the activities that can do precisely that: chorus, physical education, recess, and anything else that involves movement, play, and other forms of joyful engagement."
— Bessel A. van der Kolk

It's possible to enrol your child in an activity for every day of the week during the school year, and for every week of the summer in camps and activities. It's possible to send them to friends' houses or willing family members' houses all the time for babysitting or playdates. It's possible to use every available respite opportunity. It's possible to use volunteer drivers to transport them to every access visit. It's possible to manufacture a life in which you barely engage with your child. There are countless options to outsource your child if they are feeling difficult and unmanageable to you. Often these activities and camps are financially covered if your child is in foster care. However, in the long run, this is most likely not cultivating the consistency, healing, attachment, identity, belonging, trust, stability, and security your child so deeply needs from you, from the home, and from the family. The child you are caring for needs you, your presence, your consistency.

Photo by Cody Robinson

Reflection

What ways have you found that help your child to move from fight, flight, or freeze?

What ways have helped you to move from fight, flight, or freeze?

What activities or routines have helped or might help your child?

What activities or routines have helped or might help you?

Supporting Regulation

What physical activity do you enjoy?

What hobby do you enjoy?

What activity do you enjoy?

Do that with your child or family regularly.

What physical activity do they enjoy?

What hobby do they enjoy?

What activity do they enjoy?

Do that with your child or family regularly.

Journal

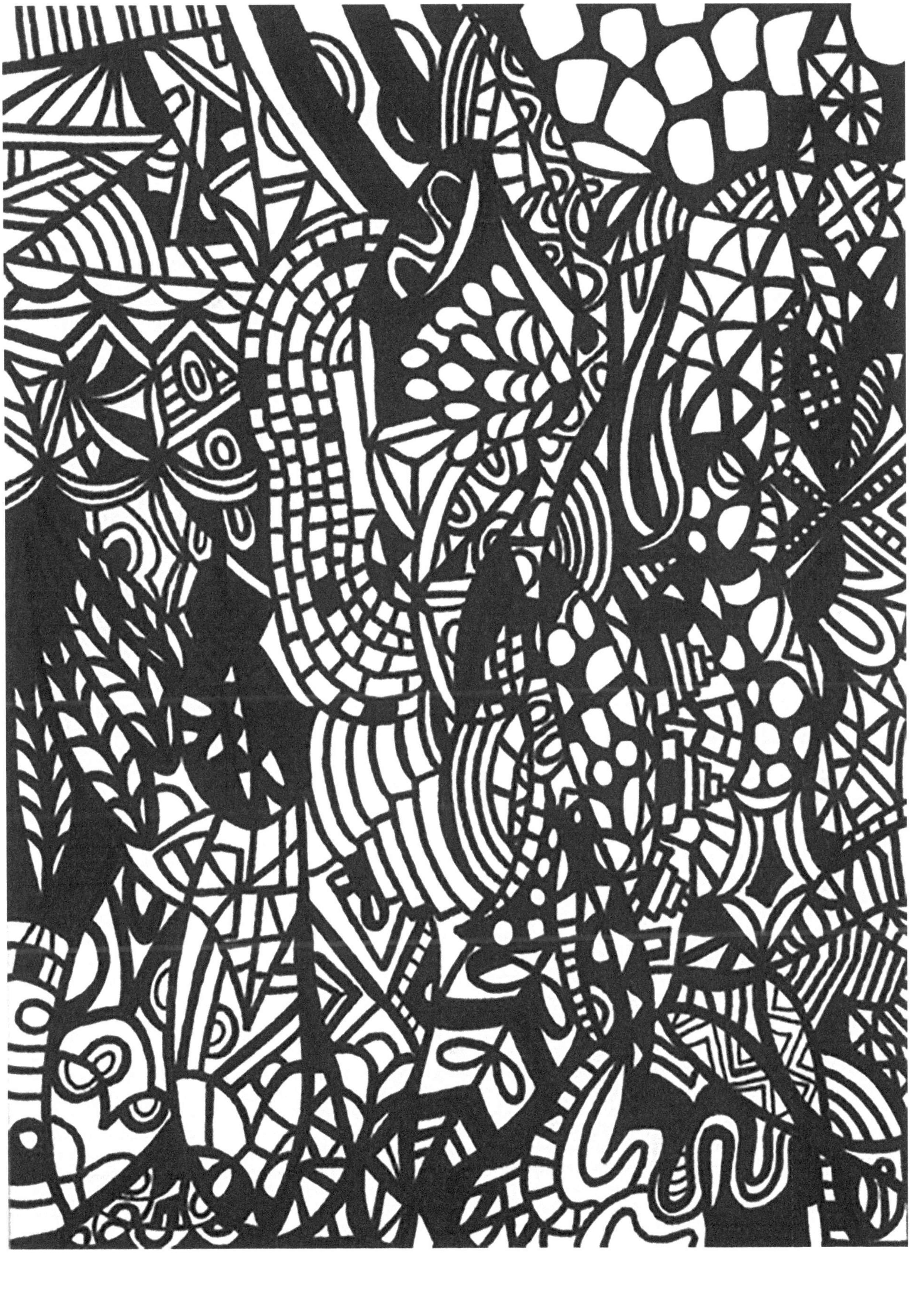

"All of us, but especially children, need such confidence—confidence that others will know, affirm, and cherish us."
— Bessel A. van der Kolk

Depending on where your child is at with physical touch, modify and grow this relationship daily to meet their needs. Even if this feels awkward or unnatural or it seems they don't need this, keeping taking small steps with them. Every person needs healthy physical touch from parents and loved ones. Take small consistent actions every day to provide safe, gentle touch. This could mean putting your hand on their back, playing with their hair, putting your arm around their shoulders, holding hands, cupping their face, giving hugs, etc. Pair these actions with communication of your care for them, reminding them of how special they are to you. Seek to build their confidence, security, and knowing that they are cherished by you. If they are seeking inappropriate physical affection with you, and you need to keep things safe for them and for you, use clear communication. Explain why that action is not appropriate and then redirect their affection to something appropriate. Instead of this being an awkward or shaming moment, use as a modelling moment. Teach them what is safe and unsafe touch between an adult and a child.

Photo by Cody Robinson

Reflection

How do you show your child you want to know them?

In what ways do you affirm your child verbally and nonverbally?

How do you show your child you cherish them?

Supporting Regulation

Cheer on your child regularly while consistently reminding yourself and them what specifically you love about them. Tell your child about the quirks that make them unique and special. Tell your child about their natural talents and gifts. Remind them how much you like them. Gush over them often. Laugh with them. Be goofy with them. Ask yourself every day: "Have I enjoyed my child today? Have I shown them or shared with them how much I like them?" If you are having a hard time liking or loving your child, or if you feel like you are constantly just getting them in trouble, then build intentional time into the day for one-to-one positive times to do something you both enjoy. Take the pressure off of managing difficult behaviours or conflict. The only priority today is to enjoy them.

Journal

"We start learning these ways of regulating our feelings from the first moment someone feeds us when we're hungry, covers us when we're cold, or rocks us when we're hurt or scared. But if no one has ever looked at you with loving eyes or broken out in a smile when she sees you; if no one has rushed to help you (but instead said, 'Stop crying, or I'll give you something to cry about'), then you need to discover other ways of taking care of yourself. You are likely to experiment with anything—drugs, alcohol, binge eating, or cutting—that offers some kind of relief."
— Bessel A. van der Kolk

One phrase we say regularly in our family is "That is a parent's job, not a child's job." This is an intentional part of our family's language. For children who have not experienced parent/child roles in a healthy way, this is new learning. This reinforces what is a parent's responsibility and not the child's. Often, roles have been confused in our children's lives. We have seen the use of this phrase to bring about enormous healing, recovery, and attachment. This can all bring about great healing in children who have been in a parenting role from a young age. Teaching a child the difference between a parent's job and a child's job allows them the freedom to be a child and trust that they will be parented. They may behave younger than their age at times since they may be re-experiencing parts of childhood that were missed. They may begin catching up.

Photo by Cody Robinson

Reflection

How has your child had to take care of themselves or others before coming to your home?

How would you describe their ability to regulate since being with you?

How have you supported their regulation? What could you try to do to support their regulation?

Supporting Regulation

Once your child has calmed down in an escalated situation, and it feels like the right time, speak slowly, hold them, hold their hand, or sit close to them to talk through the "hard time" they just had. Remind them that you are with them. They are not alone, you love them, and you still think they are amazing. Allow them to feel the security of unconditional support. If they hurt you or hurt someone else during their hard time, talk through the need for an apology and maybe a consequence to help them learn to make a different choice next time. If they hurt themselves, help them to problem-solve ways to reach out for help before it gets to that point next time. Remind them that it's okay to make mistakes and that they are learning what to do when they feel hard things. If you feel very affected negatively by their hard time, it may be important for you to take some space after they are calm. You may need to recover.

Communicate your need for space in an age-appropriate way: "We just had a very hard time. I need to take some space now and calm my body down. I'm going to take a nap, colour a picture, read a book, go take a shower, phone my friend, etc." Think of a manageable length of time they can cope with you taking some space, and then communicate that or set a timer. When you re-engage with your child, communicate that your body is calm now and move back into connection doing something good for both of you. I find this to be deeply valuable learning for children. They get to see through experience and modelling that every person is responsible for tending to their own body's feelings, reactions, cues, and needs in healthy and appropriate ways.

JOURNAL

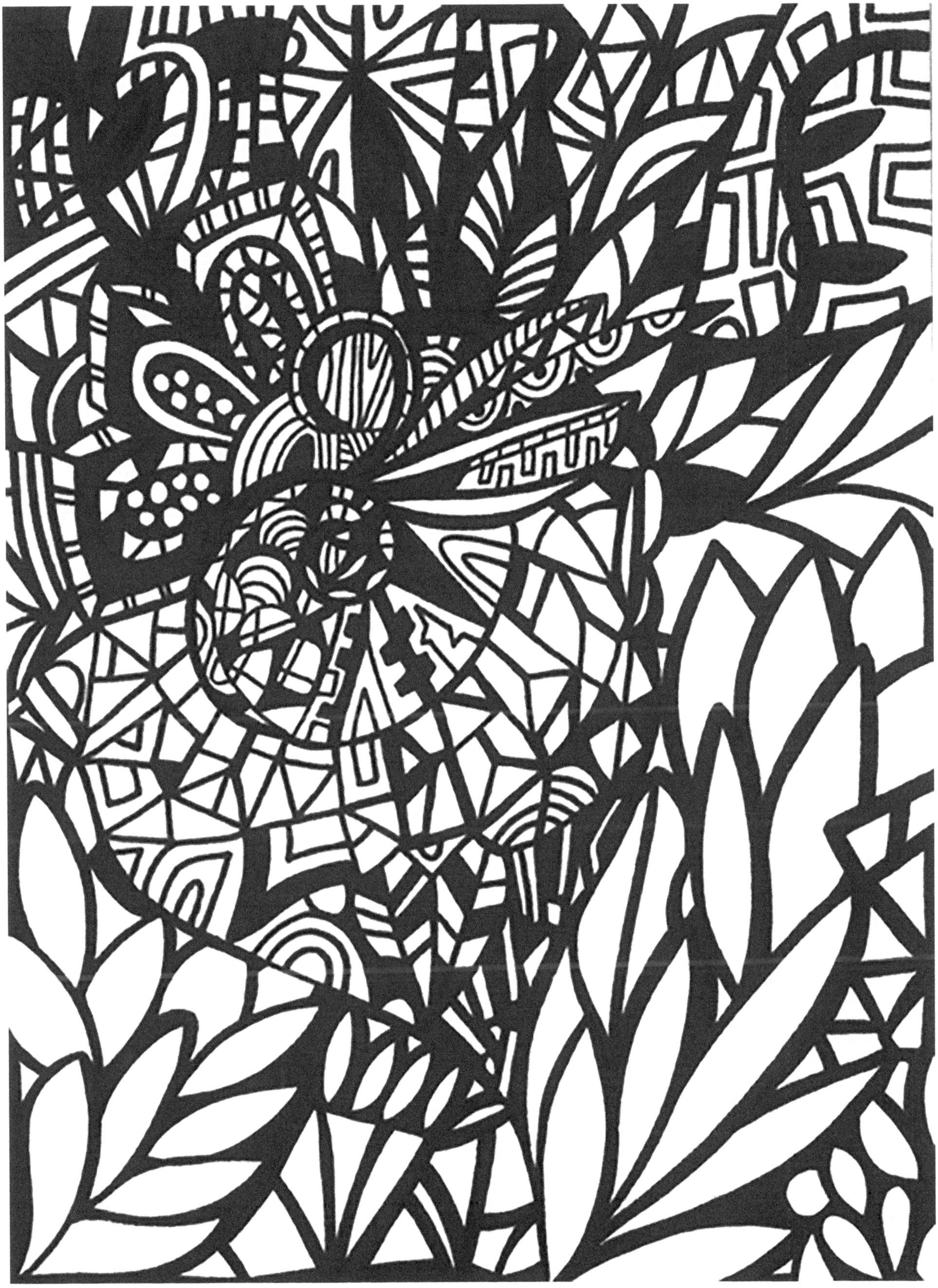

Expect your child's past memories to surface in unpredictable, random, and sometimes confusing ways. They may share parts of their story in bits and pieces when it comes up naturally for them. These are ways that typically feel manageable, healthy, and appropriate for where they are at. When this happens, simply be ready to hear them, mirror their tone, and respond simply, trying not to add new trains of thought. Let them take the conversation where they want to go, not where you may feel an urgency or curiosity to go. They are not typically looking for follow-up questions from you at this time. Instead, they may simply need space to share something on their mind that they want you to know about them and their story. More often than not, they will transition to something else more quickly than you would like, and you will need to move on with them too.

Reflection

How does your child navigate pain? Do they draw near or pull back?

How do you navigate pain typically? Do you draw near or pull back?

How does your child share their pain with you?

If that hasn't happened, how might you build those opportunities into the day in case your child needs your presence in their pain?

Supporting Regulation

Come up with a few questions to ask your child regularly to give them an opportunity to share with you. A few ideas:

What would you like to tell me today?

Is there anything you want me to know about you today?

What feels good for you today?

What feels hard for you today?

What are some of your feelings today?

Journal

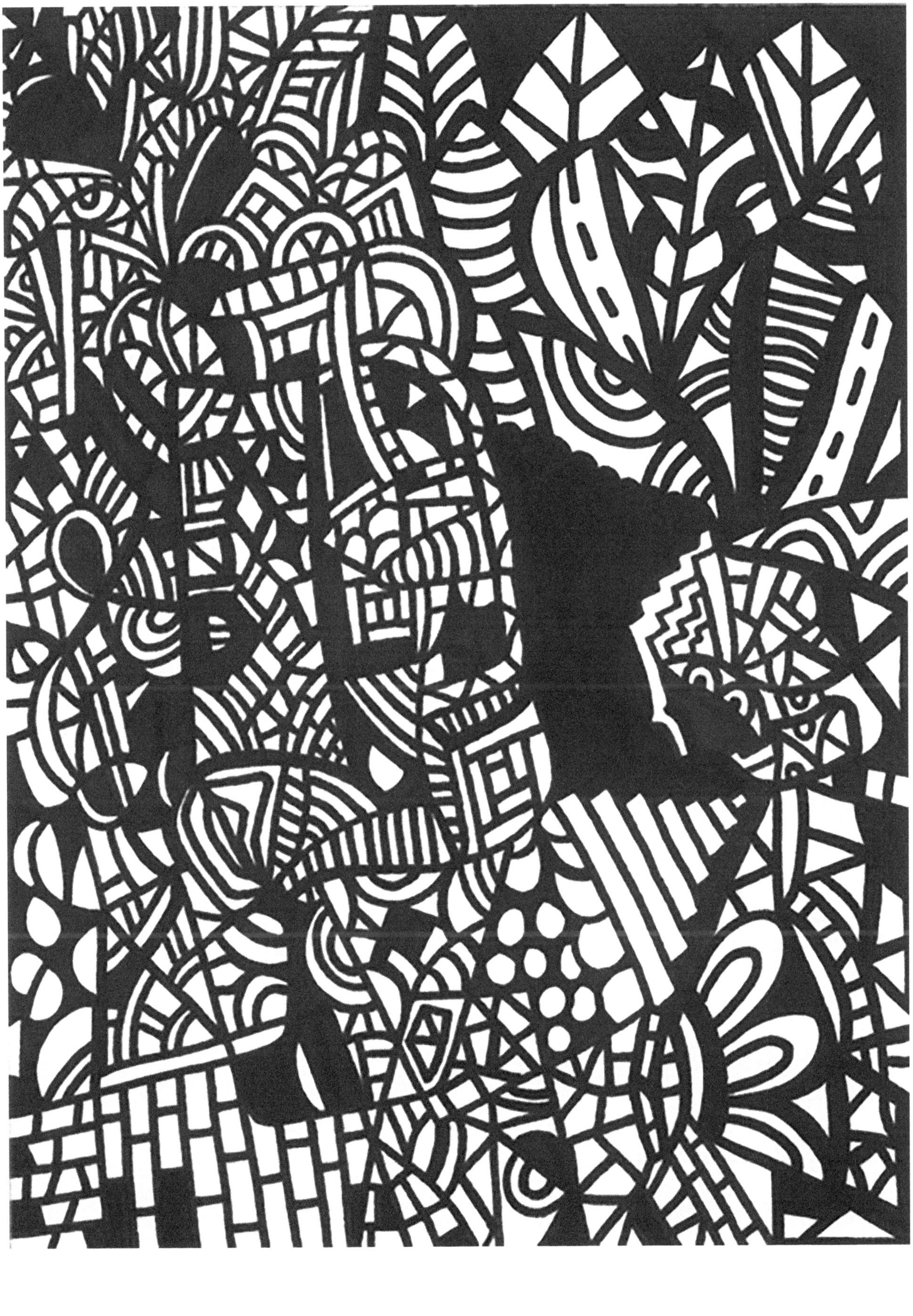

The way you parent your child at the beginning does not need to be the way you parent them long term. The sole focus in the emergency beginning phase is helping them to feel safe in whatever ways are possible for them. This phase is not normal life or normal parenting. They don't know you and you don't know them yet. This phase is not about setting up opportunities for growth, discipline, challenge, rule-following, respect, or behaviour management. This phase is simply helping the child feel safety. As they grow out of the emergency phase into more safety, trust, attachment, and belonging, you will be able to challenge them by encouraging personal growth and development. Look for small manageable opportunities of challenge throughout the day to help them to experience their ability to overcome, support their body, and move through difficulty or struggle. This builds such confidence and growth and trust for themselves. By this point, their triggers are a little more predictable for you.

Examples of triggers:
Dressing for the day

Being told no

Losing a privilege

Being given a consequence

Mealtime

Access visits

Worker visits

Court dates

Schedule change

Appointments

Grocery store

Car seat

Body temperature

Emotions of others around them

Bedtime

Morning

Putting on outdoor clothing and footwear

Loud noises

Overstimulating environments

Spilling or making a mess

Cleaning up toys or a mess

Conflict with a friend, a teacher, or a family member

Being touched

Homework

Create your own list of your child's triggers. In ways that feel manageable, encourage them to move through the distressing moment of a trigger, even if they are crying or yelling when this trigger comes up and you want to react by helping. Be present during the hard moment. Gently encourage them by telling them that you would like them to try to decide what to do instead of deferring to you. Remind them in the moment how they can help their body handle distress. This will begin building self-agency. You can communicate that they have the tools needed; they are not helpless. They do not need to fear the rising tide of their body's sensations; they can move through it. This will take great attunement from you, parent, as you discern the point at which you try this with your child. Decide when are they are able to handle some of their own triggers independently, and when they need you to intervene.

Photo by Cody Robinson

Reflection

What are some of the ways you would love to see your child grow?

To encourage growth, how can you intentionally allow challenges?

How is difficulty, struggle, or challenge spoken of in your home?

Are there any changes that need to be made in the home to provide opportunities for growth?

Supporting Regulation

Give your child an age-appropriate chore or chores to complete a few times a week during a "chores time" where the whole family works together as a team.

Depending on where they are at and what their experience has been with chores, do chores together until you feel they are confident enough and able to do them on their own. This encourages and reinforces that they are part of a family; they are a needed and valuable member. This provides your child with a sense of ownership over the space. This helps them to look outside of themselves to see how they can help others and contribute to the home.

JOURNAL

"After all, one of the defining elements of a traumatic experience—particularly one that is so traumatic that one dissociates because there is no other way to escape from it—is a complete loss of control and a sense of utter powerlessness. As a result, regaining control is an important aspect of coping with traumatic stress."
— Bessel A. van der Kolk

If your child is prone to dissociating or spacing out, look for ways to connect to them during these times. Hold and rock them and speak reassuring words of affirmation, love, and safety. Speak softly and rhythmically. If holding them isn't an option, try to maintain some physical touch. Place your hand securely on their back, either still or patting. Hold their hand, play with their hair, lie beside them, look into their eyes. Sing softly to them, read a story out loud, or run the tap in the kitchen sink. If they will let you, carry them while looking outside a window together. Go outside and look at something beautiful together. Stay with them and be patient until they "come back" to you and to the moment. Sometimes they will just snap out of it and not even be aware they were dissociating. Move on with them. Other times they may need to talk through what happened and what triggered their spacing out.

Photo by Cody Robinson

Reflection

In what moments of your child's life have they had no control?

What are some ways you see them wanting control over themselves or their life currently?

What are some things in their daily life you can allow them some control and choice over?

What ways do you seek to control your child? Are there any ways you may need to let go of control as their parent?

Supporting Regulation

As much as possible, provide two choices for most things as your child moves throughout the day.

"Would you like to wear sweatpants or jeans?"

"Would you like to eat cereal or toast?"

"Would you like to go on a hike or play at the park?"

"Would you like to give a hug or a high five?"

"Do you want to walk or be carried?"

"Do you want to shower or take a bath?"

"Do you want cuddles or space?"

"Do you want to say sorry or continue taking some space?"

If your child is having a hard time choosing one of the options, you can let them know you will give them space until they are ready to make a choice. Go into the next room and begin working on a task such as the laundry or the dishes. Calmly remind them to let you know when they have made a choice. If needed, set a timer and let them know you will be choosing if they haven't made up their mind by the time the timer goes off.

Your child has most likely had a lack of control over many parts of their lives. Allow them to grow in making choices and owning their choices when at all possible.

Journal

Your family routine may need to dramatically change based on where your child is at. For a short period of time or a long period of time, you may need to reorganize and reorder your life and priorities around your child's needs. This could look like:

- Not going out in the evenings; reinforcing a very predictable bedtime routine
- Implementing a very structured morning routine, even if that is not the nature of your family rhythms previously
- Saying no to extracurricular activities
- Not having people outside your immediate family over to your home
- Not doing as many activities or outings outside the home and neighbourhood environment
- Keeping home time very calm, relaxed, and predictable
- Staying more on top of housekeeping and prioritizing minimalism
- Slowing things way down

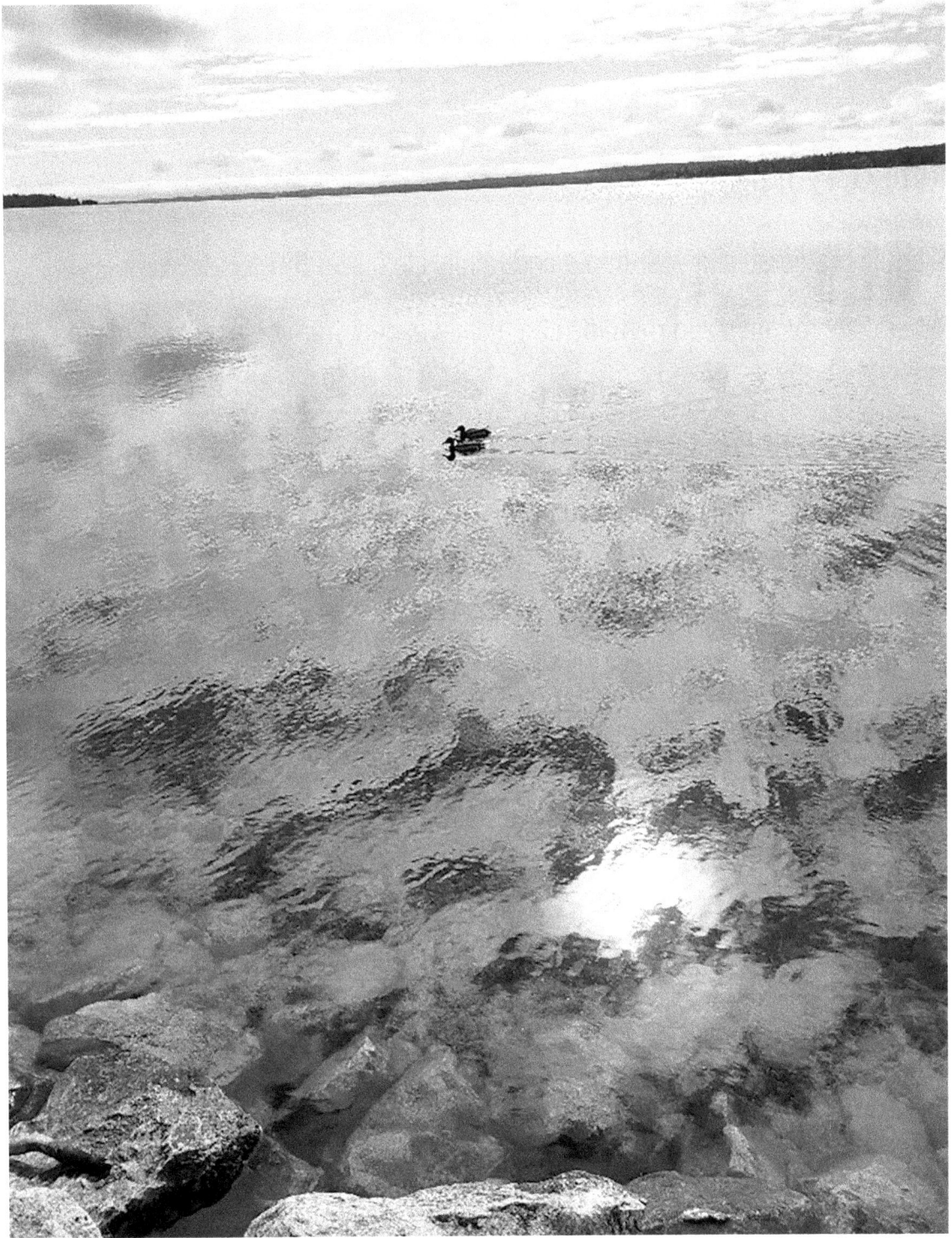

Photo by Cody Robinson

Reflection

What is predictable in your home and family life currently?

What daily routines and rhythms can a child expect from being a part of your family?

How do you provide stability as a parent?

How does your family provide stability?

How do you demonstrate that you are a supportive person?

Supporting Regulation

When you behave negatively as a parent either toward your child or around your child, be an example of respecting them, following the same calming, de-escalating strategies and language.

"I need to calm my body down right now."

"I need to take a little bit of space to calm down; I'm feeling very frustrated and upset right now."

"I need to take a break from talking for a little bit so I can help myself make better choices."

Once you have reached a place of calm, get on your child's level, look in their eyes, and apologize clearly. Use simple predictable language. "I'm sorry for how I treated you when I was upset. Please forgive me. That was not right. I will try to do better next time." Create space for openness and honesty. Ask how your negative behaviour affected them or made them feel. Ask them if they need to take some space from you to recover from that hard time. This is an important step even if they seem okay, have reconnected with you, and are ready to move on. This teaches them to slow down when they have been wronged, to check in with their body and feelings, to communicate and have difficult conversations. This is a good practice in acknowledging that parents and adults make mistakes too, not just kids.

Journal

Checklist Before Welcoming a Child

(Use if helpful or create your own)

Why have you chosen as a family to welcome this specific child?

What is your unconditional commitment as a family to this specific child?

As a family, come up with a united vision for how you want your home and family to feel to this specific child.

Is there time to purge your home of excess items before they come to create more space and simplicity for them?

Are there support people who can help you? or a cleaning service you can arrange to clean and organize your home to set everyone up for a smooth transition?

Can meal plans be lined up in advance? Can the kitchen be fully stocked?

Reflection

How do you want your home to feel to you, your family, and your friends?

What are some words you could use regularly to describe your home?

How do you see your home impacting your family positively or negatively?

Do any changes need to be implemented regularly in restoring order to your home in the areas of housework, chores, clutter, or mess?

How do you see you child's room impacting them positively or negatively?

Do changes need to be implemented regularly in restoring order to your child's room?

Supporting Regulation

Find a sustainable housecleaning system that works for you and your family. Keep exploring different organizational and cleaning methods that you can build into your weekly routine until you find one that works well. Mess, clutter, and disorganization can cause any person to feel heightened distress or dysregulation.

Journal

"When children are oppositional, defensive, numbed out, or enraged, it's also important to recognize that such 'bad behaviour' may repeat action patterns that were established to survive serious threats, even if they are intensely upsetting or off-putting."
— Bessel Van der Kolk

Photo by Cody Robinson

My sister, who is an adoptive mother, taught me early on in my parenting journey the phrase "Collect and direct." She taught me that when children are demonstrating some of their worst and most off-putting behaviours, instead of pushing them away and creating more distance, look for ways to "collect them." Intentionally bring them closer before you even approach their behaviour, even if you need to wait a day or two. This may look like rewarding negative behaviours, but this way tends to preserve and prioritize the relationship over the behaviour. Once you have re-established close connection with them, then refocus attention on "directing" them by teaching, creating a new boundary, talking through a consequence, debriefing, and helping them find a way forward with them feeling attached to you.

Some "collecting" ideas:

Take your child out of school or cancel any plans and have a special day together (movies, painting pottery, park, hike, swimming, etc.).

Carve out some special home time for the two of you (crafts, reading, spa time, movie, baking, games, etc.).

Plan a weekend getaway away for you and your child, or the whole family.

REFLECTION

What are your child's consistently negative behaviours?

In what ways do those negative behaviours indicate past survival or past coping?

SUPPORTING REGULATION

If you are a foster parent and you feel that overnight respite or babysitting is a need for you, try asking a family member or a close friend if they would be willing to commit to being the consistent home your child goes to when outside care is needed. They will need to be approved by your social worker. It will greatly benefit your child to have fewer transitions while building trust and consistent felt safety with the same caregiver.

Journal

"Children sense — even if they are not explicitly threatened — that if they talked about their beatings or molestation to teachers they would be punished. Instead, they focus their energy on not thinking about what has happened and not feeling the residues of terror and panic in their bodies. Because they cannot tolerate knowing what they have experienced, they also cannot understand that their anger, terror, or collapse has anything to do with that experience. They don't talk; they act and deal with their feelings by being enraged, shut down, compliant, or defiant. Children are also programmed to be fundamentally loyal to their caretakers, even if they are abused by them. Terror increases the need for attachment, even if the source of comfort is

ALSO THE TERROR. I HAVE NEVER MET A CHILD BELOW THE AGE OF TEN WHO WAS TORTURED AT HOME (AND WHO HAD BROKEN BONES AND BURNED SKIN TO SHOW FOR IT) WHO, IF GIVEN THE OPTION, WOULD NOT HAVE CHOSEN TO STAY WITH HIS OR HER FAMILY RATHER THAN BEING PLACED IN A FOSTER HOME."
— BESSEL A. VAN DER KOLK

It is important to acknowledge with your child and for yourself the attachment they have often shared with their birth family members. Sometimes it can be easy to just label them as harmful people, people they shouldn't be with. This may be true in some cases. However, sometimes it's not that black and white. Your child may have had some good, meaningful, and significant experiences in their first homes, with their first families. This can be uncomfortable, painful, or hard for us as foster or adoptive parents to acknowledge because we feel protective. However, this will be very important for your child to have a full understanding of how they have been loved and cared for in their past. This will support successful reunification, if at all possible. If not possible, this will support their identity and understanding of their history and story, and this will make good connections possible moving forward.

Photo by Cody Robinson

Reflection

How would you describe your child's relationship to their birth parents and birth siblings?

How would you describe your relationship to your child's birth parents and birth siblings?

Do you have a desire to build healthy, positive relationship with any of your child's birth family members? Why or why not?

Supporting Regulation

If your child has access visits with their birth parents or birth siblings, make an effort to get to know them and understand who they are as individuals and how your child engages in relationship with them. Seek to support and affirm the relationship. Be the drop-off and pick-up instead of using a volunteer driver. Practise humility, gentleness, and kindness within these complex and sometimes awkward relationships. Though it may be uncomfortable, complicated, or painful for you or for them, this will add a depth of support and care for your child. Keep a simple routine of comfort and zero expectations for your child after visits. Offer comfort food, comfort items, and a calm environment to and from visits. Put a movie on or allow them extra screen time. Make yourself present and available if you are needed, or give them space if that is what they need for their body to come back down.

Journal

"Having a biological system that keeps pumping out stress hormones to deal with real or imagined threats leads to physical problems: sleep disturbances, headaches, unexplained pain, over-sensitivity to touch or sound. Being so agitated or shut down keeps them from being able to focus their attention and concentration. To relieve their tension, they engage in chronic masturbation, rocking, or self-harming activities (biting, cutting, burning and hitting themselves, pulling their hair out, picking at their skin until it bleeds). It also leads to difficulties with language processing and fine motor coordination. Spending all their energy on staying in control, they usually have trouble paying attention to things like schoolwork, that

ARE NOT DIRECTLY RELEVANT TO THEIR SURVIVAL, AND
THEIR HYPERAROUSAL MAKES THEM EASILY DISTRACTED."
— Bessel A. van der Kolk

If you notice or are aware of your child engaging in habits of self harm, rocking/any repetitive movement, or self stimulation, how can you move them toward health and safety gently without just trying to get them to stop that habit?

Create a boundary of safety for them if they want to self-stimulate. Regardless of their age, they need to know this cannot be practised around other people. Talk openly and without shaming language. Let them know this is private and they need privacy when they would like to do this, such as by having alone time in the bathroom or in their bedroom.

Involve yourself if they are rocking and repeating a movement. Try holding them and rocking back and forth, or maintaining a form of physical touch that they are okay with.

Try to keep sensory items, fidgets, or distraction activities on hand you can pass to them when they are wanting to self-harm. Sit with them and try doing the activity with them. Sometimes they will resist the option. If that is the case, just maintain closeness and physical contact if possible until they are ready to stop and move on.

Photo by Cody Robinson

Journal

"Traumatized people live with seemingly unbearable sensations: they feel heartbroken and suffer from intolerable sensations in the pit of their stomach, or tightness in their chest. Yet avoiding feeling the sensations in our bodies increases our vulnerability to being overwhelmed by them. Body awareness puts us in touch with our inner world, the landscape of our organism. Simply noticing our annoyance, nervousness, or anxiety immediately helps us shift our perspective and opens up new options other than our automatic, habitual reactions."
— Bessel A. van der Kolk

We use the phrases "Listen to your body" or "I'm listening to my body" every day in our home. We prioritize tuning in and helping our children learn to listen to, respond to, and communicate their physical sensations. We have seen this to be very healing, freeing, and confidence-building. We celebrate when we notice our child listening and responding to their body, and we also seek to model this pattern as parents. We often ask questions to help our children tune into their bodies when they are unsure.

Some ideas to begin building this into your family language:

Bathroom habits: "Great job listening to your body and letting us know you have to go to the bathroom."

Food: "Great job listening to your body and letting me know you're hungry and need a snack.

Clothing: "Great job listening to your body and changing into something more comfortable."

Sensory: "Tell me why you don't you like the way your pants are fitting around your waist."

"What do you like about that cool breeze coming through the window?"

"Tell me why you don't like the feeling of sand stuck on your feet."

We can't always move from discomfort to comfort right away. We can't always provide comfort right away for our kids. We can however choose how we respond to their physical cues and sensations. We could say, "Thanks for letting me know your body is hungry. We need to be patient a little longer for dinner to be on the table."

Photo by Cody Robinson

Journal

Dear Parent,

As foster or adoptive parents, may we stay fiercely committed to the children who come into our homes and families no matter what. For however long we get to parent our children – short term, long term, or forever – may our hearts consistently return to tender, even in moments and seasons of overwhelming hardship, grief, or loss. May we seek to have humility in our families when we make mistakes along the way. May we apologize and repair well when we fail each other. May our families grow, heal, and thrive together. May we remain steadfast in our unconditional love and support for one another. May our greatest desire as parents be that our children would know to their core that who they are is lovable, likeable, and wanted, even in the midst of challenging behaviours, diagnoses, trauma reactions, and circumstances beyond their control. If you would benefit from further connection please give me a call, send me an email, or follow me on

Instagram. I would love to explore how I can be an ongoing support to you as you parent. I am certified in provide coaching, and I would love to be part of your team in this way.

Jess

Ongoing Connection:
Phone: 647-773-2643
Instagram: @foster.adoptive.parenting
Email: robinsonfosterfamily@gmail.com

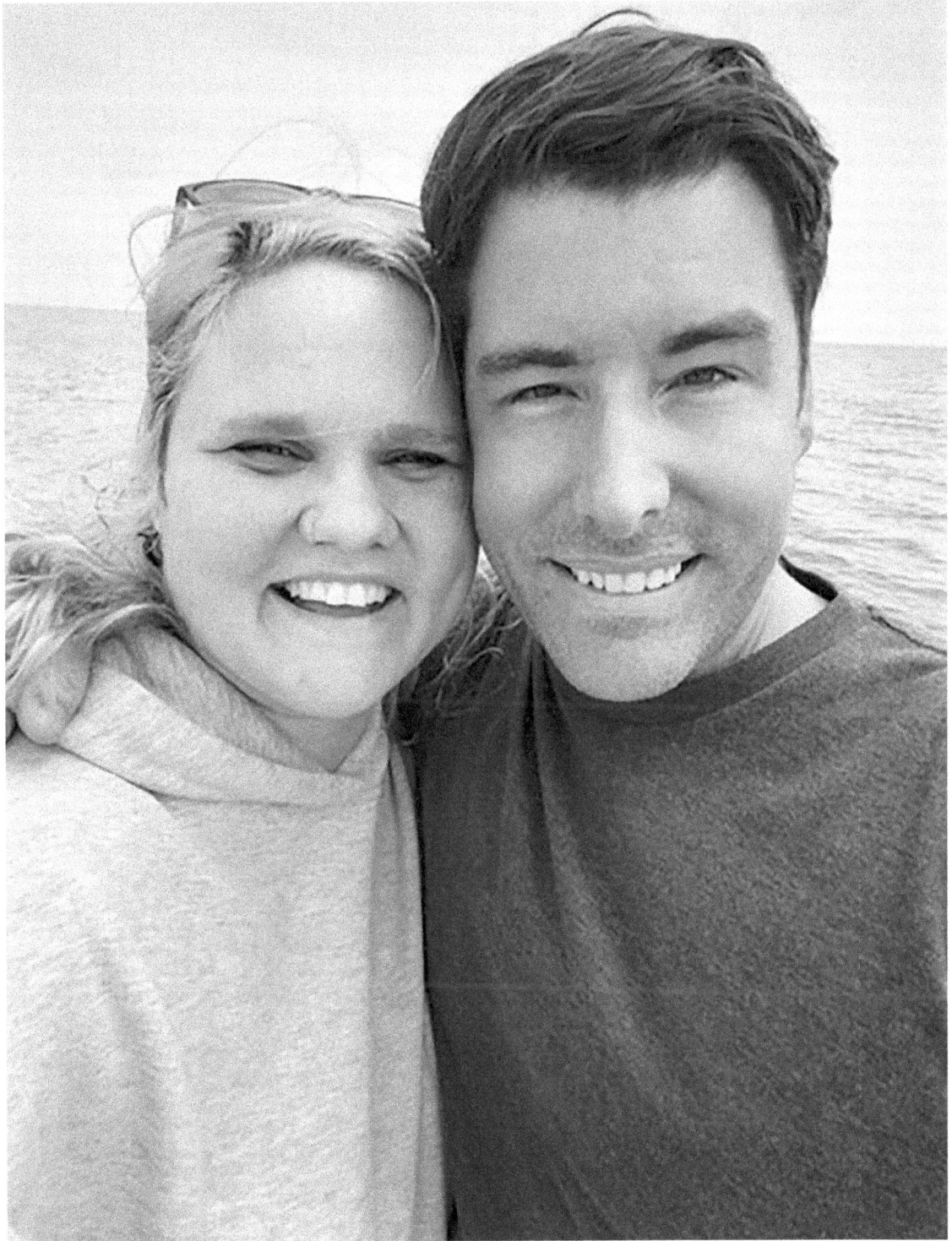

Photo by Cody Robinson

Milton Keynes UK
Ingram Content Group UK Ltd.
UKHW051852151223
434483UK00008B/223

9 780228 895633